The Little Book of Spiritual Wisdom

Natalie

on the occasion of our
2nd anniversary, I am so
happy and proud to have
found this with you. Also I
delight every day in having
the honour of calling you my
wife. Natalie, thank you! from the
bottom of my heart.
                    I Love you
                    your very happy husband

THE LITTLE BOOK OF
SPIRITUAL
WISDOM

Compiled by Philip Law

A LION BOOK

This edition copyright © 1998 Lion Publishing

Published by
Lion Publishing plc
Sandy Lane West, Oxford, England
www.lion-publishing.co.uk
ISBN 0 7459 4063 3

First edition 1998
10 9 8 7 6 5 4 3 2 1 0

Acknowledgments
We would like to thank all those who have given us permission to include material in this book. Every effort has been made to trace and acknowledge copyright holders of all the quotations in this book. We apologize for any errors or omissions that may remain, and would ask those concerned to contact the publishers, who will ensure that full acknowledgment is made in the future.

A catalogue record for this book is available from the British Library

Printed and bound in Great Britain by Caledonian International Book Manufacturing, Glasgow

The only way to get our values right is to see, not the beginning, but the end of the way, to see things, not in the light of time, but in the light of eternity.

WILLIAM BARCLAY

The very best and utmost attainment in this life is to remain still and let God act and speak in thee.

MEISTER ECKHART

We must not be disturbed at our imperfections, since for us perfection consists in fighting against them.

FRANÇOIS DE SALES

The Longest Journey
is the Journey Inwards.

Dag Hammarskjöld

Though God be everywhere present,
yet he is only present to thee in the
deepest and most central part of thy soul.

WILLIAM LAW

IF YOU WISH TO BE FULLY ALIVE YOU MUST
DEVELOP A SENSE OF PERSPECTIVE. LIFE IS
INFINITELY GREATER THAN THIS TRIFLE YOUR
HEART IS ATTACHED TO AND WHICH YOU HAVE
GIVEN THE POWER TO SO UPSET YOU.

ANTHONY DE MELLO

To live is to change,
and to be perfect is
to have changed often.

JOHN HENRY NEWMAN

*Poverty of mind as a spiritual attitude
is a growing willingness to recognize the
incomprehensibility of the mystery of life.
The more mature we become the more we will
be able to give up our inclination to grasp, catch,
and comprehend the fullness of life and the
more we will be ready to let life enter into us.*

HENRI NOUWEN

Purpose is what gives life a meaning... A drifting boat always drifts downstream.

CHARLES H. PARKHURST

In the rush and noise of life, as you have
intervals, step within yourselves and be still.
Wait upon God and feel his good presence; this
will carry you through your day's business.

WILLIAM PENN

Every day the choice
between good and evil
is presented to us in simple ways.

W.E. SANGSTER

IT IS THE CRUSHED GRAPE THAT YIELDS THE WINE.

ANONYMOUS

Hope is hearing the melody of the future. Faith is to dance it.

RUBEM ALVES

He who knows himself,
knows everyone.
He who can love himself,
loves everyone.

St Antony

We are undefeated as long as we keep on trying, as long as we have some source of movement within ourselves and are not just moved by outside forces, as long as we retain the freedom of right decision and action, whatever the circumstances.

GEORGE APPLETON

No man can do properly what he is called upon
to do in this life unless he can learn to forget
his ego and act as an instrument of God.

W.H. AUDEN

God is an infinite circle
whose centre is everywhere
and whose circumference is nowhere.

St Augustine

A wise man will make more
opportunities than he finds.

FRANCIS BACON

BEAUTY MAY BE SAID TO BE GOD'S TRADE MARK IN CREATION.

HENRY WARD BEECHER

The pride of the peacock is the glory of God.
The lust of the goat is the bounty of God.
The wrath of the lion is the wisdom of God.
The nakedness of woman is the work of God.

WILLIAM BLAKE

If you are wise you will show yourself rather as a reservoir than a canal. For a canal spreads abroad the water it receives, but a reservoir waits until it is filled before overflowing, and thus shares without loss to itself its superabundance of water.

St Bernard of Clairvaux

a God who let us prove his existence would be an idol.

DIETRICH BONHOEFFER

We know that God is everywhere; but certainly we feel his presence most when his works are on the grandest scale spread before us; and it is in the unclouded night-sky, where his worlds wheel their silent course, that we read clearest his infinitude, his omnipotence, his omnipresence.

CHARLOTTE BRONTË

The true way to be humble is not to stoop until you are smaller than yourself, but to stand at your real height against some higher nature that will show you what the real smallness of your greatness is.

PHILLIPS BROOKS

Modesty is to merit
what shade is to
figures in a picture;
it gives strength and
makes it stand out.

JEAN DE LA BRUYÈRE

In the spiritual journey we travel through the night towards the day. We walk not in the bright sunshine of total certainty but through the darkness of ignorance, error, muddle and uncertainty. We make progress in the journey as we grow in faith.

CHRISTOPHER BRYANT

Mere silence is not wisdom,
for wisdom consists in knowing
when and how to speak and
when and where to keep silent.

JEAN-PIERRE CAMUS

WE ARE MIRRORS OF GOD, CREATED TO
REFLECT HIM. EVEN WHEN THE WATER
IS NOT CALM, IT REFLECTS THE SKY.

ERNESTO CARDENAL

The only way to have
a friend is to be one.

RALPH WALDO EMERSON

NO GIFT IS MORE PRECIOUS THAN GOOD ADVICE.

DESIDERIUS ERASMUS

He who would do good to another
must do so in minute particulars.

WILLIAM BLAKE

*An atheist is a man who has
no invisible means of support.*

HARRY EMERSON FOSDICK

Facing the darkness, admitting the pain, allowing the pain to be pain, is never easy. That is why courage — big-heartedness — is the most essential virtue on the spiritual journey.

MATTHEW FOX

Solitude is essentially the discovery
and acceptance of our uniqueness.

LAWRENCE FREEMAN

Without sacrifice there is no resurrection. Nothing grows and blooms save by giving. All you try to save in yourself wastes and perishes.

André Gide

Never, for the sake of peace and quiet,
deny your own experience or convictions.

DAG HAMMARSKJÖLD

KINDNESS IS IN OUR POWER,
BUT FONDNESS IS NOT.

SAMUEL JOHNSON

Many persons have a wrong idea of what constitutes true happiness. It is not attained through self-gratification but through fidelity to a worthy purpose.

HELEN KELLER

Make a rule, and pray to God to help you
to keep it, never, if possible, to lie down at
night without being able to say, I have made
one human being at least a little wiser, a
little happier, or a little better this day.

CHARLES KINGSLEY

His divinity is understood as the power of the future making our present appear in a new light. The future is God's: which means that, wherever the individual human being goes, in life or death, God is there.

HANS KUNG

Hypocrisy is the homage
which vice pays to virtue.

FRANÇOIS, DUC DE LA ROCHEFOUCAULD

WE ARE BORN HELPLESS. AS SOON AS WE ARE
FULLY CONSCIOUS WE DISCOVER LONELINESS.
WE NEED OTHERS PHYSICALLY, EMOTIONALLY,
INTELLECTUALLY; WE NEED THEM IF WE ARE
TO KNOW ANYTHING, EVEN OURSELVES.

C.S. LEWIS

I was angry with my friend;
I told my wrath, my wrath did end.
I was angry with my foe;
I told it not, my wrath did grow.

WILLIAM BLAKE

What is Time? The shadow on the dial, the striking of the clock, the running of the sand, day and night, summer and winter, months, years, centuries – these are but arbitrary and outward signs, the measure of Time, not Time itself. Time is the Life of the soul.

Henry Wadsworth Longfellow

WHEN YOU GIVE, SEE THAT
YOU GIVE THAT WHICH
MULTIPLIES IN GIVING.

RAYMOND LULL

True peace is not merely
the absence of tension;
it is the presence of justice.

MARTIN LUTHER KING

Age is not all decay; it is the ripening,
the swelling, of the fresh life within,
that withers and bursts the husk.

GEORGE MACDONALD

Anxiety comes from strain, and strain is caused by too complete a dependence on ourselves, on our own devices, our own plans, our own idea of what we are able to do.

THOMAS MERTON

IF A MAN'S DEEDS ARE NOT IN HARMONY WITH HIS PRAYER, HE LABOURS IN VAIN.

ABBA MOSES (DESERT FATHER)

PROGRESS IN THE SPIRITUAL LIFE
COMES FROM CLIMBING A LADDER
OF WHICH THE RUNGS ARE MADE
ALTERNATELY OF BELIEF AND DOUBT.

EDWARD PATEY

Be careful to preserve your health. It is a trick of the devil, which he employs to deceive good souls, to incite them to do more than they are able, in order that they may no longer be able to do anything.

VINCENT DE PAUL

Suffering passes;
having suffered never passes.

CHARLES PÉGUY

Eternity is not something
that begins after you are dead.
It is going on all the time.
We are in it now.

CHARLOTTE PERKINS GILMAN

Thankfulness is a soil in which
pride does not easily grow.

MICHAEL RAMSEY

*Wisdom is nine-tenths
a matter of being
wise in time.*

THEODORE ROOSEVELT

In every man there is something of the Universal Spirit, strangely limited by that which is finite and personal, but still there. Occasionally it makes itself known in a word, look or gesture, and then becomes one with the stars and sea.

MARK RUTHERFORD

ONE PERSON WORKS
UPON ANOTHER PERSON
FROM OUTSIDE INWARDS,
BUT GOD ALONE COMES TO US
FROM WITHIN OUTWARDS.

JAN VAN RUYSBROECK

JOYS IMPREGNATE,
SORROWS BRING FORTH.

WILLIAM BLAKE

Perfection is being not doing;
it is not to effect an act
but to achieve a character.

FULTON JOHN SHEEN

Wisdom is the right use of knowledge. To know is not to be wise... There is no fool so great as the knowing fool. But to know how to use knowledge is to have wisdom.

CHARLES HADDON SPURGEON

If your morals make you dreary,
depend upon it they are wrong.

ROBERT LOUIS STEVENSON

Never be ashamed to own you have been in the wrong, 'tis but saying you are wiser today than you were yesterday.

JONATHAN SWIFT

One who stands beside the sea sees the infinite ocean of the waters, but cannot grasp the extent of them, beholding only a part. So it is with one who is judged worthy to fix his gaze in contemplation on the infinite ocean of God's glory and behold him with the intelligence: he sees not how great God is, but only what the spiritual eyes of his soul can grasp.

SYMEON THE NEW THEOLOGIAN

WHATEVER WE DO THAT CREATES DEADNESS IS A SIN.

JOHN V. TAYLOR

The most satisfactory thing in life is to have been able to give a large part of oneself to others.

PIERRE TEILHARD DE CHARDIN

I am a part of all that I have met.

ALFRED, LORD TENNYSON

IT IS BY FORGIVING
THAT ONE IS FORGIVEN.

MOTHER TERESA

You never know yourself until you
know more than your body. The
image of God is not sealed in
the features of your face, but
in the lineaments of your soul.

THOMAS TRAHERNE

A spiritual life is simply a life in which all that we do comes from the centre, where we are anchored in God: a life soaked through and through by a sense of his reality and claim, and self-given to the great movement of his will.

EVELYN UNDERHILL

*All fanaticism is a strategy
to prevent doubt from
becoming conscious.*

H.A. WILLIAMS

Solitude permits
the mind to feel.

WILLIAM WORDSWORTH

A MAN CAN BE SO BUSY
MAKING A LIVING THAT HE
FORGETS TO MAKE A LIFE.

WILLIAM BARCLAY

God is the beyond
in the midst of life.

DIETRICH BONHOEFFER

*The pilgrim who spends all his time
counting his steps will make little progress.*

JEAN-PIERRE CAMUS

No one can know God who has not first known himself. Go to the depths of the soul, the secret place of the Most High, to the roots, to the heights; for all that God can do is focused there.

MEISTER ECKHART

Call on God,
but row away
from the rocks.

RALPH WALDO EMERSON

FRUITLESS IS THE WISDOM
OF HIM WHO HAS
NO KNOWLEDGE OF HIMSELF.

DESIDERIUS ERASMUS

Nothing is so strong as gentleness,
nothing so gentle as real strength.

FRANÇOIS DE SALES

TRUTH WHICH IS MERELY TOLD
IS QUICK TO BE FORGOTTEN;
TRUTH WHICH IS DISCOVERED
LASTS A LIFETIME.

WILLIAM BARCLAY

All that is sweet, delightful, and amiable in this world, in the serenity of the air, the fineness of seasons, the joy of light, the melody of sounds, the beauty of colours, the fragrancy of smells, the splendour of precious stones, is nothing else but Heaven breaking through the veil of this world, manifesting itself in such a degree and darting forth in such variety so much of its own nature.

WILLIAM LAW

Forgiveness is not an occasional act,
it is a permanent attitude.

MARTIN LUTHER KING

Every painful event contains in itself
a seed of growth and liberation.

ANTHONY DE MELLO

Growth is the only evidence of life.

JOHN HENRY NEWMAN

Most of our human emotions are closely related to our memory. Remorse is a biting memory, guilt is an accusing memory, gratitude is a joyful memory, and all such emotions are deeply influenced by the way we have integrated past events into our way of being in the world.

HENRI NOUWEN

Laws of nature are God's thoughts thinking themselves out in the orbits and the tides.

CHARLES H. PARKHURST

In this world, things that are naturally
to endure for a long time,
are the slowest in reaching maturity.

VINCENT DE PAUL

Believe nothing against another, but upon good authority; nor report what may hurt another, unless it be a greater hurt to others to conceal it.

WILLIAM PENN

All personality has a radiation.
The radiations of those in whom
God dwells are mighty
beyond measurement.

W.E. SANGSTER

What is a saint? A particular individual completely redeemed from self-occupation; who, because of this, is able to embody and radiate a measure of eternal life.

EVELYN UNDERHILL

A man there was,
though some did count him mad;
the more he cast away the more he had.

JOHN BUNYAN

Goodness is something so simple:
Always live for others, never to seek
one's own advantage.

DAG HAMMARSKJÖLD

HE WHO SEES THE INFINITE IN ALL THINGS, SEES GOD.

WILLIAM BLAKE